Workbook

For

How to Carry What Can't Be Fixed

A Journal for Grief

(An Interactive Guide To Megan Devine's Book)

Dailia Pages

Copyright © [2023] by [Dailia Pages]

Table Of Contents

How to Use the Workbook

Welcome to Megan Devine's "How to Carry What Can't Be Fixed: A Journal for Grief" companion workbook. This workbook is intended to be your companion and guide as you travel through the deep experience of loss, providing you with a structured and introspective space to explore your feelings, insights, and healing.

1. Starting Out:
- Read the Book: Before entering into this workbook, Megan Devine's "How to Carry What Can't Be Fixed" is highly recommended. The book contains essential insights and teachings that will lay the groundwork for your workbook experience.

- Create a Supportive Environment: Locate a quiet and comfortable area where you can concentrate on your reflections and activities without distractions. Keep a journal, a pen, and the book itself close for reference.

2. How to Use the Workbook:

- Follow the Chapter Order: The workbook is organized in the same way as the main book. Because each chapter corresponds to a distinct area of the book, it's better to read them in order. Begin with Part 1: Departure and progress to Part 3: Return.

- Self-Reflection Questions: At the end of each chapter in this workbook, there are self-reflection questions related to the book's teachings and material. These questions are intended to elicit introspection and self-awareness. Take your time thinking about and responding to these questions.

- Self-Evaluation and writing: In addition to self-reflection questions, the workbook includes self-evaluation prompts and writing exercises. These activities are designed to help you delve deeper into your emotions, thoughts, and experiences.

3. Your Individual Journey:
- No Correct or Incorrect Answers: Keep in mind that there are no correct or incorrect answers in this workbook. Your mourning journey is deeply personal and one-of-a-kind. Feel free to express yourself honestly and without judgement.

- Take Your Time: Grieving is a natural process that takes its time. There is no haste, and mending takes its time. Be kind with yourself and allow your emotions to emerge organically.

4. Additional Information:

- Seeking Professional Help: While this workbook is a great tool for self-reflection and healing, it's crucial to identify when you need professional help. If your grieving becomes overpowering or uncontrolled, consider seeking help from a therapist or counselor.

5. Final Thoughts:

- Honoring Your Loved One: As you work through this workbook, keep in mind that you are honoring your loved one and your relationship with them. It's an opportunity to process your feelings, remember them, and find meaning in your mourning.

- Accepting Your Growth: Grief is about more than simply loss; it is also about growth and transformation. In the middle of your sadness, embrace the opportunity to learn about yourself, uncover your resilience, and find a new sense of purpose.

Quick Synopsis

"In 'How to Carry What Can't Be Fixed: A Journal for Grief, ' author Megan Devine provides a compassionate and practical guide for those navigating the difficult terrain of grief, drawing on personal experience and professional expertise to help readers confront the profound and often overwhelming emotions that accompany loss. "

The book is divided into three parts: departure, adventure (of sorts), and return, and takes readers on a transformative journey through the various stages of grief. Devine's approach is refreshingly honest, recognizing that grief is not something to 'fix, ' but rather a lifelong companion that can be carried with grace and understanding.

Devine shares personal experiences, insights, and vital lessons acquired from her own grief journey throughout the book, giving readers the skills they need to explore their feelings, seek assistance, and find moments of comfort despite the suffering.

The book is a journal for self-reflection and healing, with self-reflection questions, self-evaluation prompts, and practical exercises to help readers navigate their unique grief journeys. Devine emphasizes that there is no 'one-size-fits-all' approach to grieving, and she empowers readers to define their own path and timeline for healing.

Part 1: DEPARTURE

Chapter 1: The Story Begins

Key Lessons

1. Acceptance of truth: Grief begins with acceptance of the truth of loss. It is critical to accept suffering and heartache as part of the healing process.

2. The Unpredictable Path: Grief is an emotional rollercoaster that does not follow a linear path. Learn that having good and bad days is normal, and that there is no right or wrong way to grieve.

3. Sharing Vulnerability: Sharing your sorrow story with someone you trust can be a crucial step toward healing. Vulnerability has the potential to promote connection and support.

4. Grieving Is Individual: Each person's grieving experience is unique. Comparing your grief to that of others can lead to feelings of resentment and loneliness. Accept your own journey.

5. The Power of Words: Putting your feelings into words might help you make sense of your loss. Writing and discussing your emotions can be helpful.

Self reflection questions

1. Have you truly embraced the fact of your loss,   and are you allowing yourself to recognize the significant shift it has brought to your life?

_____

_____

_____

_____

_____

_____

2. How do you negotiate the unpredictability of loss while acknowledging that your emotions will shift over time?

_____

_____

_____

_____

_____

_____

3. Who in your support network can you lean on and share your loss with, allowing yourself to be vulnerable and forging bonds through shared pain?

_____
_____
_____
_____
_____
_____

4. Throughout your mourning journey, how have you used language to communicate and describe your emotions? Are there any words or phrases that ring true for you?

_____
_____
_____
_____
_____
_____

5. How has sharing your sorrow story with trustworthy friends or writing helped you heal?

_____

_____

_____

_____

_____

_____

Chapter 2: What If I Refuse?

Key Lessons

1. Grieving Resistance: It is natural to oppose grieving since it is painful. However, resisting it can cause the healing process to take longer.

2. Grief as a Companion: Grief will accompany you for a long time, if not forever. Instead of fighting it, learn to coexist with it and discover methods to bring it with you.

3. The Physical Cost: Grief can emerge physically. Recognize the effect it has

on your body and take care of yourself both physically and mentally.

4. Seeking Professional Help: Grief can be overwhelming at times, and seeking professional help is a brave step toward healing.

5. Allow yourself to experience a wide range of emotions, including anger, guilt, and grief. These feelings are normal during the grieving process and must be acknowledged.

Self reflection questions

1. Have you encountered opposition to recognizing your grief, and if so, what specific components of it do you find difficult to accept?

---

2. How do you see grief as a companion for life rather as something to "get over, " and how has this influenced your healing journey?

---

3. Have you seen any physical signs of grieving, and how do you prioritize self-care in order to deal with them?

4. What measures have you taken to seek professional treatment or support when your grief has become overwhelming?

5. As part of your grieving process, how have you given yourself permission to feel a wide range of emotions, such as anger, sadness, guilt, and moments of relief or happiness?

Chapter 3: Getting By with a Little Help-Real and Imagined

Key Lessons

1. Lean on Your Support System: Seek peace and comfort from friends and relatives who genuinely care about your well-being.

2. Creativity as a Coping Mechanism: Creating art, music, or writing can provide a therapeutic outlet for your feelings.

3. Rituals and customs can help you honor your loved one while also providing a sense of connection and continuity.

4. Even if your loved one is no longer alive, imagine them as a source of support and advice in your life. This can be reassuring.

5. Self-Compassion: Exercise self-compassion by treating yourself with the same love and sympathy that you would extend to a grieving friend.

Self reflection questions

1. How do you value the presence of friends and allies in your life who provide unflinching support during your mourning journey?

2. How do you cope with your sorrow through artistic hobbies, and how have these outlets helped you manage your emotions?

3. What significant rituals or traditions have you established to honor your loved one's memory, and how do they add to your sense of connection and continuity?

_____

_____

_____

_____

_____

_____

4. In what ways have you imagined your loved one's support, even in their absence, and how has this mental connection provided comfort and strength?

_____

_____

_____

_____

_____

_____

5. How do you exercise self-compassion
   and guarantee that you treat yourself
   with care and understanding as you go
   through the grieving process?

_____

_____

_____

_____

_____

_____

Chapter 4: The Inside View

Key Lessons

1. Investigate Your Inner World: Grief is more than simply outward emotions of sadness. Allow yourself time to explore your inner thoughts and feelings, even if they are uncomfortable.

2. Unresolved Issues: Grief can bring unresolved issues with the deceased or your connection with them to the surface. Recognize and, if feasible, work through these.

3. Dreams and recollections: Dreams and recollections of a loved one might be bittersweet, but they can also provide possibilities for connection and grief processing.

4. Regular self-reflection can help you better comprehend your grief journey as well as your growing relationship with the person you've lost.

5. Seeking Meaning: Look for meaning in your grief. Understanding the meaning or influence of your loved one's life can be reassuring at times.

Self reflection questions

1. How do you explore your inner thoughts, worries, and feelings about grieving, and are there any particular areas that you find difficult to confront?

2. Have you encountered unsolved difficulties or silent emotions along your mourning journey, and how do you deal with them when they arise?

3. What role did your loved one's dreams and recollections play in your grieving process, and how do you pay attention to and understand these experiences?

4. How can you use self-reflection and introspection to better understand your grief journey and your changing relationship with a loved one?

5. What meaning have you found in your bereavement experience, as well as the legacy and influence of your loved one's life?

_____

_____

_____

_____

_____

_____

_____

Chapter 5: This All Hurts

Key Lessons

1. Accepting Pain: Recognize that pain is an inevitable component of the grieving process. It's okay to be sad, and it shows how much you cared for your loved one.

2. Physical Symptoms of grieving: Recognize the physical effects of grieving on your body, such as tiredness, headaches, or stomachaches.

3. Grief Waves: Grief frequently comes in waves, which might be unexpected. Learning to ride these waves and recognize their presence can be beneficial.

4. Patience with Yourself: Be gentle with yourself as you work through the grief of loss. It takes time to heal, and there is no rush to "get over" pain.

5. Grief can bring you together with those who have also suffered loss. It can be extremely healing to share your suffering with those who understand.

Self reflection questions

1. How have you accepted grief's agony as an essential part of your journey, realizing that it is a reflection of your love and connection with the person you've lost?

   _____

   _____

   _____

   _____

   _____

   _____

   _____

2. Have you seen any bodily signs of grief? How do you ensure your physical health and well-being?

   _____

   _____

   _____

   _____

   _____

   _____

3. How do you negotiate the emotional waves of sorrow, both the acute pain and the relatively calm?

_____
_____
_____
_____
_____
_____

4. Are you being patient with yourself as you face the obstacles of loss, understanding that healing takes time and that setbacks are a natural part of the process?

_____
_____
_____
_____
_____

5. How has sharing your grief with others who have experienced loss helped you find connection and validation, and how has this sharing influenced your grief experience?

_____

_____

_____

_____

_____

_____

Part 2: ADVENTURE (OF SORTS)

Chapter 6: Rough Roads Ahead

Key Lessons

1. Accept Uncertainty: Grief frequently leads to an uncertain future. Accept the uncertainty, knowing that life will never be the same again, but it can still have worth and purpose.

2. The Effects of Grief on Relationships: Recognize that mourning can damage relationships with those who may not

fully understand your situation. Communication is essential.

3. Self-Care Is Required: In difficult circumstances, self-care is not a luxury but a requirement. Make taking care of your physical and emotional well-being a priority.

4. Grief Has the capacity to Transform You and Your Life: Grief has the capacity to transform you and your life. Investigate how it has influenced your perspective, priorities, and values.

5. The Long-Term Journey: Grief is a life-changing event that can last a

lifetime. Develop long-term plans and coping methods while acknowledging that healing is ongoing.

Self reflection questions

1. How do you deal with unanticipated problems that arise during your grief journey, and are there any particular obstacles that you find particularly difficult to overcome?

2. What activities do you engage in to maintain your physical and mental well-being, and how do you prioritize self-care as a crucial aspect of navigating the difficult roads of grief?

3. Have you actively sought aid and support when going through particularly difficult periods in your grief journey, and what sorts of services have been most helpful to you?

_____

_____

_____

_____

_____

_____

4. In what ways do you recognize your limitations and set boundaries to maintain your mental and emotional health while grieving?

_____

_____

_____

_____

_____

_____

5. How do you accept the ebb and flow of grief, realizing that your feelings may fluctuate in strength from day to day, and how does this knowledge influence your coping strategies?

_____

_____

_____

_____

_____

_____

Chapter 7: Rest and Restoration

Key Lessons

1. Rest is essential since grieving can be exhausting. Recognize the importance of rest, both physical and emotional, in restoring your vitality.

2. Mindfulness and Presence: Being mindful and present in the moment can help you cope with the overwhelming feelings that sorrow can bring.

3. Spending time in nature can bring solace and a sense of connection,

helping you to find moments of serenity in the midst of loss.

4. Remembering a Loved One: Find meaningful ways to commemorate and respect your loved one. Make rituals or traditions to commemorate their life.

5. Balancing Grief and Joy: It is acceptable to have moments of joy or laughter while grieving.

Self reflection questions

1. What techniques do you employ to ensure you get the rest you need? How do you prioritize rest and restoration as vital components of your mourning journey?

2. Have you sought calm and consolation in the midst of grief's upheaval, and how can these times contribute to your emotional renewal?

3. What efforts have you done to create a safe and comfortable physical location where you can recharge emotionally?

_____
_____
_____
_____
_____
_____

4. How have you dealt with any guilt you may have felt about taking time for yourself, realizing that self-care is an essential part of the healing process?

_____
_____
_____
_____
_____
_____

5. What tactics do you use to deal with overwhelm during your grief journey, and how do you balance your obligations with self-care practices?

_____

_____

_____

_____

_____

_____

_____

Chapter 8: The Gifts and Perils of Distraction

Key Lessons

1. Understanding Distraction as a Coping method: Recognize that distraction can be a helpful coping method at times, bringing relief from overwhelming grief.

2. Distractions: Differentiate between helpful (hobbies, interests) and unhealthy (substance abuse, avoidance) distractions that may impede healing.

3. Distraction and Guilt: Avoid feeling guilty about finding distraction when necessary. It is a legitimate method of dealing with pain and emotions.

4. Balancing Distraction and Processing: While distraction can be useful, don't overlook the significance of grieving and processing your feelings.

5. Self-Compassion in Distraction: Use self-compassion when employing distraction to cope with sadness. Recognize it as a temporary solution rather than a long-term one.

Self reflection questions

1. In your grief journey, how do you strike a balance between distraction as a beneficial coping tool and a potential means of avoidance?

_____

_____

_____

_____

_____

_____

2. How do you practice mindfulness when distracted, ensuring that you remain fully present in the moment?

_____

_____

_____

_____

_____

_____

3. Have you identified when distraction becomes avoidance, and how do you confront this shift in your coping strategies?

4. How do you find healthy, positive distractions that bring you joy and comfort, and how do they contribute to your overall well-being?

5. How do you honor your emotions and
   allow yourself to return to your grief
   when you're ready, without judgment
   or self-criticism?

_____

_____

_____

_____

_____

_____

Chapter 9: Anger Deserves Its Own Chapter

Key Lessons

1. Recognize Anger: Recognize that anger is a normal aspect of the grieving process. Allow yourself to feel and express this feeling in appropriate ways.

2. Anger as a conceal: Anger can sometimes conceal other underlying feelings such as grief or fear. To address the underlying issues, investigate the source of your rage.

3. Avoid Self-Judgment: Do not judge yourself if you are angry. It's a reasonable reaction to loss, and it doesn't make you a horrible person.

4. Healthy Expression: Look for constructive outlets for your rage, such as journaling, physical activity, or talking to a trusted friend or therapist.

5. Working towards forgiveness can eventually be a powerful step in the healing process, helping you to relinquish anger and discover serenity.

Self reflection questions

1. How can you recognize and accept rage as a normal and valid feeling during your mourning journey?

_____
_____
_____
_____
_____
_____

2. Have you investigated the source of your rage, whether directed at yourself, others, or the circumstances of your loss?

_____
_____
_____
_____
_____
_____

3. What constructive channels for your rage have you discovered, and how do you express this emotion in a healthy way?

_____

_____

_____

_____

_____

_____

_____

4. In what ways have you worked toward forgiveness and letting go of deep anger, acknowledging that hanging onto anger can stymie your healing?

_____

_____

_____

_____

_____

_____

_____

5. How have you sought understanding and validation of your anger without judgment from friends, family, or support groups, and how has this sharing of feelings been helpful for you?

_____

_____

_____

_____

_____

_____

_____

Chapter 10: The Vantage Point

Key Lessons

1. Gaining Perspective: Consider how sorrow has changed your outlook on life, relationships, and what truly matters.

2. Grief can bring about self-discovery and personal growth. Take advantage of the opportunity to discover more about yourself.

3. Find a happy medium between recognizing your sadness and allowing times of joy and happiness to coexist with grief.

4. Connection to Others: Use your unique mourning viewpoint to connect with and help others who are also grieving.

5. Mindful Living: Practice mindful living by appreciating the present moment and discovering beauty and significance even when you are sad.

Self reflection questions

1. How have you acquired perspective on your grieving experience through time, and how has this influenced your recovery process?

2. What personal growth and transformation have you experienced as a result of your sorrow, and how have these changes informed your identity and values?

3. How do you reflect on your loved one's legacy and the good impact they had on your life, and how does this contemplation provide you with strength and inspiration?

_____

_____

_____

_____

_____

_____

4. Have you discovered a greater sense of purpose or a desire to make important changes in your life in memory of your loved one, and how have you gone about doing so?

_____

_____

_____

_____

_____

_____

5. How do you maintain contact with the person you've lost, and how does their memory inspire you as you move forward in life?

_____

_____

_____

_____

_____

_____

_____

Chapter 11: The Ultimate Boon

Key Lessons

1. Finding Meaning: Consider how your mourning journey can lead to a more profound sense of purpose or meaning in your life.

2. Legacy and influence: Consider how you can carry on your loved one's memory and legacy, so adding to their lasting influence.

3. Helping those: Look for ways to assist those who are grieving, as providing support can be healing in and of itself.

4. Recognize your own perseverance and strength as you endure the difficulties of mourning and emerge with renewed wisdom.

5. Continued Development: Recognize that your journey does not end with grief. Continue to grow and evolve, seeking new chances for fulfillment and growth.

Self reflection questions

1. How have you incorporated sadness into your life story, realizing that it is not about "getting over" loss, but rather about learning to live with it?

   _____
   _____
   _____
   _____
   _____
   _____
   _____

2. In what ways have you accepted grief's transformational power and acknowledged the resilience and strength it has brought to your life?

   _____
   _____
   _____
   _____
   _____
   _____

3. How can you recognize your individual grief journey and the course it has followed, while acknowledging that there is no single goal in mourning?

_____

_____

_____

_____

_____

_____

4. How have you found significance and insight in your grief, and how do you use these lessons to live a life of purpose and fulfillment?

_____

_____

_____

_____

_____

_____

5. How do you enjoy the ultimate blessing of living a life that is in line with your beliefs and objectives while grieving, and how does this balance enrich your journey?

Part 3: RETURN

Chapter 12: I Don't Want to Return to "Normal"

Key Lessons

1. Recognize that your definition of "normal" may shift as a result of grieving. Accept a new normal that respects your experiences and feelings.

2. Consider how you might reintegrate into regular life without rejecting or repressing your pain.

3. Setting limits: Set limits to protect your mental well-being while navigating the demands and pressures of "normalcy. "

4. Continue Prioritizing Self-Care: Prioritize self-care even when you return to your normal routines.

5. Flexibility in Healing: Recognize that healing is an ongoing process with no set timeline for resuming normalcy.

Self reflection questions

1. In the aftermath of your loss, how have you reevaluated the concept of "normal" in your life, and what changes have you contemplated in your search of a new normal?

2. How have you resisted society pressure to "move on" fast following a loss, and how have you kept faith in your personal mourning timeline?

3. Have you expressed your desire for a slower pace of grieving to friends, family, or your support system, and how has this communication affected your healing process?

_____
_____
_____
_____
_____
_____

4. During your journey to a new normal, how have you exercised self-compassion and enabled yourself to handle setbacks or deep grief?

_____
_____
_____
_____
_____
_____

5. What groups or support networks have you sought out that recognize and validate your decision to redefine normalcy, and how have these communities helped you feel like you belong?

Chapter 13: Your Grief, Your Way

Key Lessons

1. Individual grieving Journey: Recognize that your grieving journey is entirely unique to you. There is no correct or incorrect way to grieve, and your feelings are genuine.

2. Self-Compassion and Gentleness with Yourself: As you negotiate your grief, practice self-compassion and gentleness with yourself. Avoid self-criticism or judging yourself.

3. External Pressures: Be conscious of external pressures and expectations surrounding how you should grieve. Maintain your own needs and pace.

4. Finding Personal methods to Honor and Remember Your Loved One: Find personal methods to honor and remember your loved one that resonate with you and represent their value in your life.

5. Self-Expression: Use artistic outlets or personal rituals to express yourself and heal, allowing your emotions to find a healthy release.

Self reflection questions

1. What actions have you done to create your own path, timing, and coping techniques after recognizing that your grief journey is deeply personal and individualized?

   _____

   _____

   _____

   _____

   _____

   _____

2. How have you dealt with external expectations and judgments about how you should grieve, and how do you keep faith in your unique experience?

   _____

   _____

   _____

   _____

   _____

   _____

3. How have you developed meaningful ways to celebrate your loved one's memories that reflect your particular relationship and experiences?

_____

_____

_____

_____

_____

_____

4. Have you allowed your grieving process to evolve through time, and if so, what tactics have you used to adapt and adjust your coping mechanisms as needed?

_____

_____

_____

_____

_____

_____

5. In your mourning journey, how do
   you advocate for your own needs and
   boundaries, and how do your voice
   and choices contribute to your sense
   of agency and self-empowerment?

_____

_____

_____

_____

_____

_____

Chapter 14: Sidestepping Bad Support

Key Lessons

1. Recognize indicators of useless or poisonous support from friends and family, such as disparaging comments or pressure to move on.

2. Setting Boundaries: Learn to set boundaries with those who may unintentionally aggravate or worsen your grief.

3. Seeking Trusted Support: Surround yourself with people who truly understand and support your

mourning process, even if it involves attending support groups or going to counseling.

4. Communication: It is critical to maintain open and honest communication with loved ones. Share your requirements and boundaries clearly so that they can best support you.

5. Educating Others: Sometimes others don't know how to provide the assistance you require. Inform them about your grief and what has helped you.

Self reflection questions

1. How do you recognize unhelpful assistance and avoid people who respond negatively to your grieving, and how does this safeguard your emotional well-being?

_____
_____
_____
_____
_____
_____

2. What boundaries have you established with people who may unwittingly bring you pain or discomfort during your mourning, and how have these limits worked to preserve your mental and emotional health?

_____
_____
_____
_____
_____
_____

3. How do you actively seek out people who genuinely want to understand your pain and offer empathetic support, and how has this helped your recovery process?

_____

_____

_____

_____

_____

_____

4. Have you gone out of your way to educate friends and family on the complexity of mourning, and how has open and honest communication resulted in more meaningful support?

_____

_____

_____

_____

_____

_____

5. How have support groups or professional assistance augmented the support you receive from your immediate circle, and how have these extra resources improved your coping and healing?

_____

_____

_____

_____

_____

_____

_____

Chapter 15: Friends and Allies and Asking for Help

Key Lessons

1. Recognize the value of friends and allies who stand by your side through times of sadness, bringing comfort and strength.

2. Asking for Assistance: Don't be scared to ask for assistance when you need it. Friends and allies frequently want to help you but are unsure how.

3. Reciprocity in Friendship: Recognize that friendships are a two-way street, and it's normal to count on your

friends for support while you're mourning.

4. Energy Conservation: Be aware of your energy levels and spend time with individuals that invigorate and uplift you rather than deplete you.

5. Grief Education: Encourage friends and allies to learn more about grief so they can better comprehend your experience.

Self reflection questions

1. How do you identify the value of friends and allies who provide unshakable support during your mourning journey, and how have these people contributed to your emotional well-being?

   _____
   _____
   _____
   _____
   _____
   _____

2. In what ways do you practice mutual support, both in terms of asking for aid and offering help to others in times of grief and hardship?

   _____
   _____
   _____
   _____
   _____
   _____

3. By sharing your grief experience with trusted friends, how have you developed meaningful connections with others, and how have these ties enhanced your knowledge of your own emotions?

_____

_____

_____

_____

_____

_____

4. How can you communicate effectively and openly with those on whom you rely for help, ensuring that your requirements, boundaries, and preferences are clearly expressed?

_____

_____

_____

_____

_____

_____

5. How can you cultivate a culture of reciprocal support in your relationships, where you both ask for and give aid when required, and how does this culture improve your connections and community?

_____

_____

_____

_____

_____

_____

_____

Chapter 16: Master of Two Worlds

Key Lessons

1. Finding a means to Balance Grief and Life: Find a means to balance your grieving process with your regular life duties, realizing that they can coexist.

2. Identity Shift: Recognize that your identity may shift as you deal with your loss, and that this is normal. Accept the changing aspects of oneself.

3. Recognize your tenacity in navigating both the world of mourning and the world of everyday living.

4. Growth through Adversity: Adversity often leads to growth. Accept the possibility for personal improvement as part of your grief journey.

5. Self-Compassion: Maintain your self-compassion and self-care practices while you navigate the complexity of both your internal world of grief and your exterior world of duties.

Self reflection questions

1. How can you strike a balance between grief and daily life, enabling them to coexist rather than seeing them as distinct entities?

_____

_____

_____

_____

_____

_____

_____

2. In what ways have you included your grief into your life story, recognizing that it is a part of who you are as well as your hopes and dreams?

_____

_____

_____

_____

_____

_____

_____

3. How have you shown resilience and adaptability in dealing with both your grief and the responsibilities of daily living, and how do these traits contribute to your sense of empowerment?

4. How do you gradually resume your responsibilities and commitments while emphasizing self-care and setting reasonable goals to ensure you meet your obligations while grieving?

5. How do you routinely reflect on your growth and accomplishments as you continue to mature and adapt to the obstacles of juggling grief and daily life, and how does this reflection drive you to keep going?

Chapter 17: Freedom to Live

Key Lessons

1. Embracing Life: Allow yourself to experience joy, happiness, and fulfillment in life while still grieving.

2. Grief as a Companion: Recognize that grief and a fulfilling life can coexist.

3. Legacy and Memory: Continue to commemorate your loved one's memory in ways that add significance to your life.

4. Moving Forward: Accept the freedom to move on with your life while acknowledging that grief will always be a part of it.

5. Support and Community: Maintain contact with your support network, as they can continue to provide strength and company on your path.

Self reflection questions

1. How do you embrace life, find joy, and find meaning when grieving, and what choices have you chosen to live fully and authentically?

   _____

   _____

   _____

   _____

   _____

   _____

2. How have you honored your loved one's memory by living well and celebrating their life via your actions and choices?

   _____

   _____

   _____

   _____

   _____

   _____

3. How does the person you've lost inspire you in your daily life, and how do you identify their presence and influence in your experiences?

_____

_____

_____

_____

_____

_____

4. How do you view the legacy of love and perseverance that you have carried forward from your mourning experience, and how does sharing these traits contribute to a positive impact on your community and the world?

_____

_____

_____

_____

_____

_____

5. How do you express thanks for the moments of beauty, love, and happiness that life still provides, and how does this acknowledgement help you feel at peace and fulfilled?

Self Assessment Questions

The following questions are to help you track your progress in this book, you can answer them in your personal journal.

1. Reflection on the trip: How have you changed or progressed in your understanding of grief and capacity to handle it as a result of your trip through this workbook?

_____

_____

_____

_____

_____

_____

_____

2. Growth and Resilience: As a result of your participation in this workbook, what personal traits and attributes have you discovered or developed? How have you shown resilience in the face of grief's difficulties?

_____

_____

_____

_____

_____

_____

3. Lesson Integration: How have the book's core teachings and the self-reflection exercises in this workbook been integrated into your everyday life and attitude to grief?

_____

_____

_____

_____

_____

4. Self-Compassion and Self-Care: How have you demonstrated self-compassion and prioritized self-care along your journey? What effect has this had on your general well-being?

_____

_____

_____

_____

_____

_____

_____

5. Reflect on the support networks and connections you've established or strengthened during your mourning journey. How have these relationships aided your recovery?

_____

_____

_____

_____

_____

_____

_____

6. Challenges and setbacks: What obstacles have you encountered along the way, and how have you dealt with or learned from them?

_____

_____

_____

_____

_____

_____

_____

7. Future Development: How do you see yourself continuing to grow and heal in the future? Are there any aspects of your grief journey that you'd like to delve deeper into?

_____

_____

_____

_____

_____

_____

8. Sharing Your Insights: Have you shared your insights and experiences with others, both inside and outside of your support network? How has this sharing aided your personal healing and possibly helped others?

_____

_____

_____

_____

_____

_____

9. Seeking Professional Assistance: Have you sought professional assistance or direction during your mourning journey, if applicable? How has this additional assistance enhanced your workbook experience?

_____

_____

_____

_____

_____

10. Grief's Place in Your Life: As you near
the end of this workbook, how do you
see grief's place in your life now versus
when you started?

Made in the USA
Columbia, SC
10 July 2024